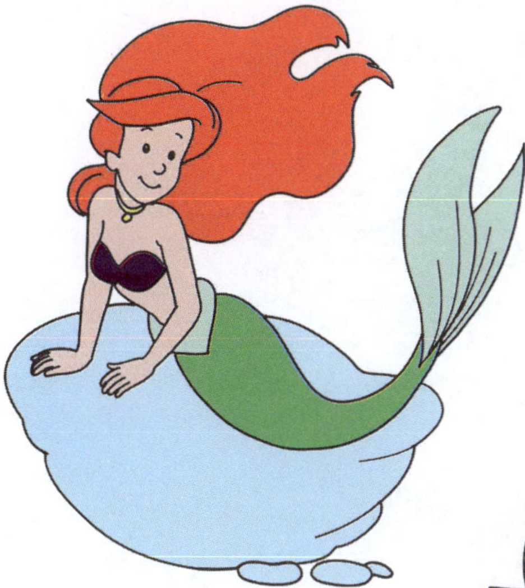

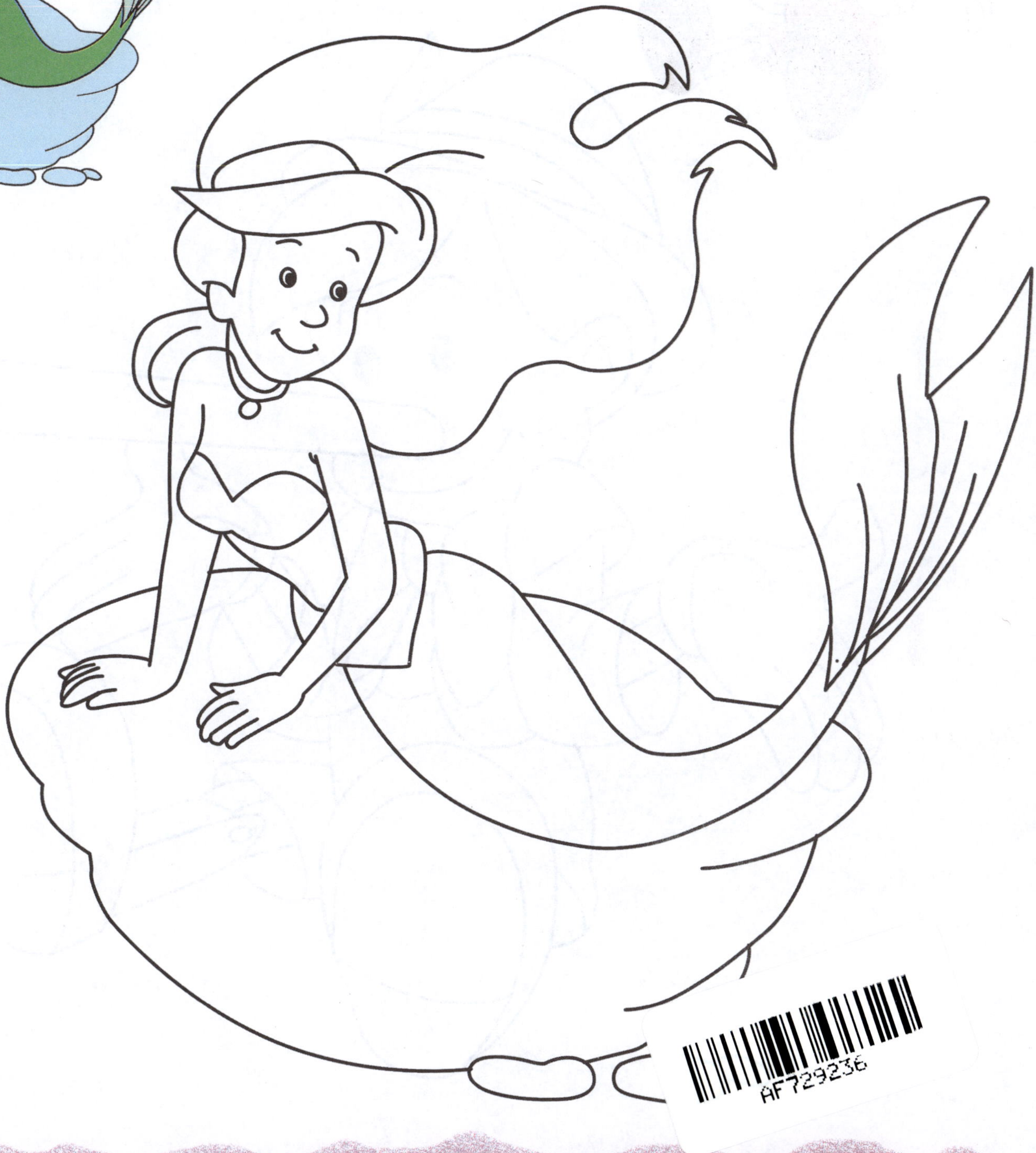

little mermaid

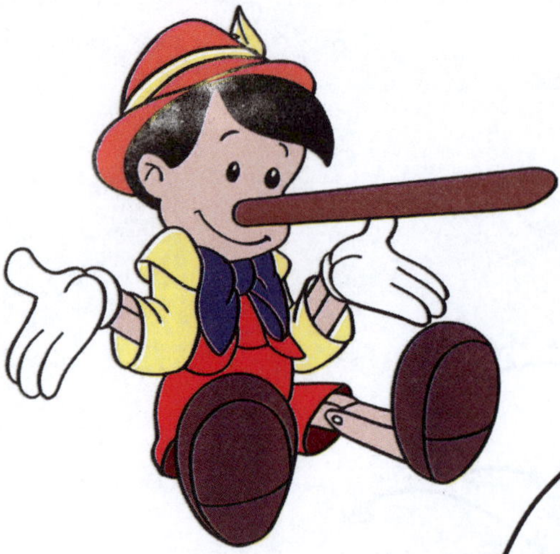

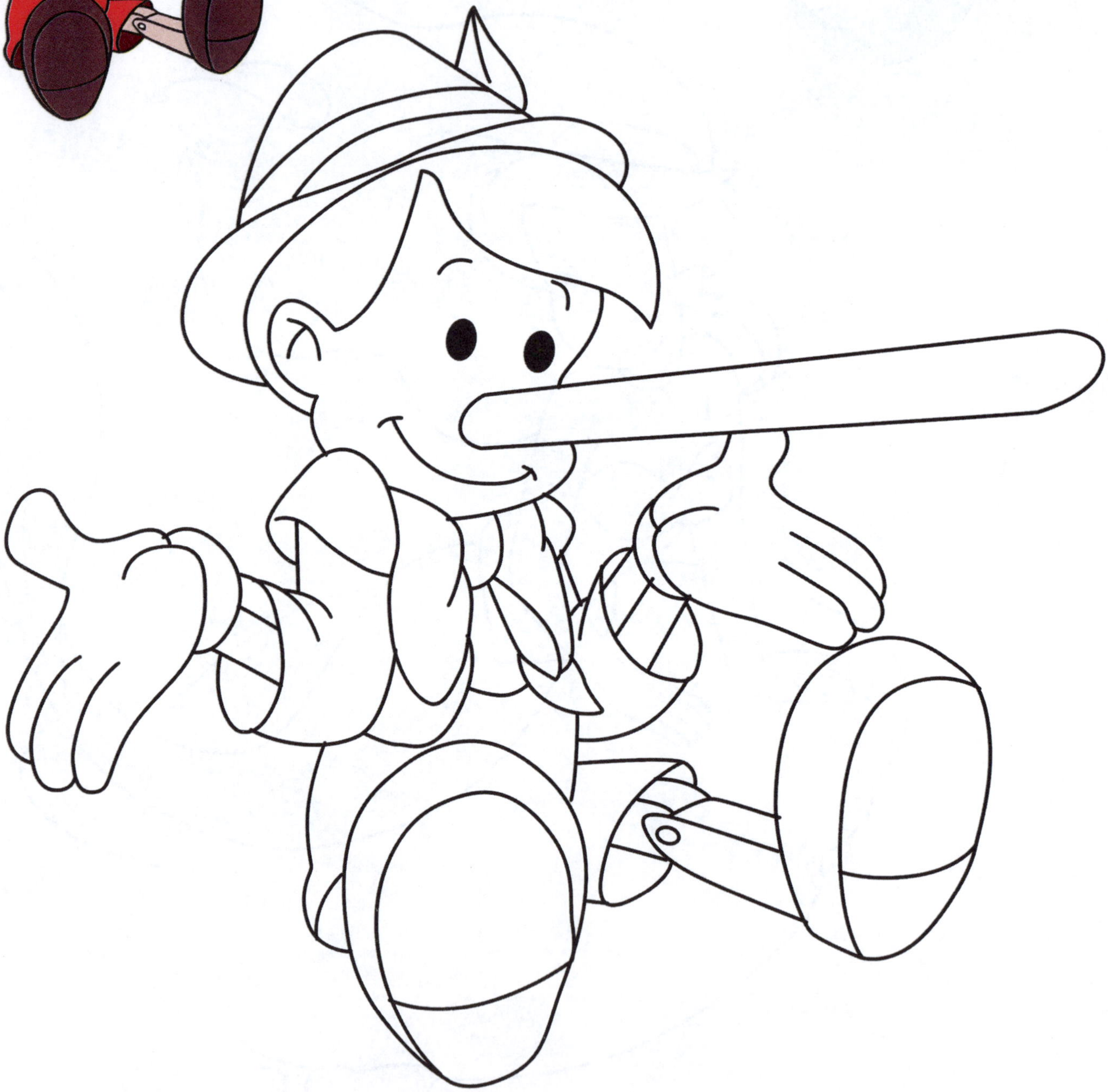

pinocchio

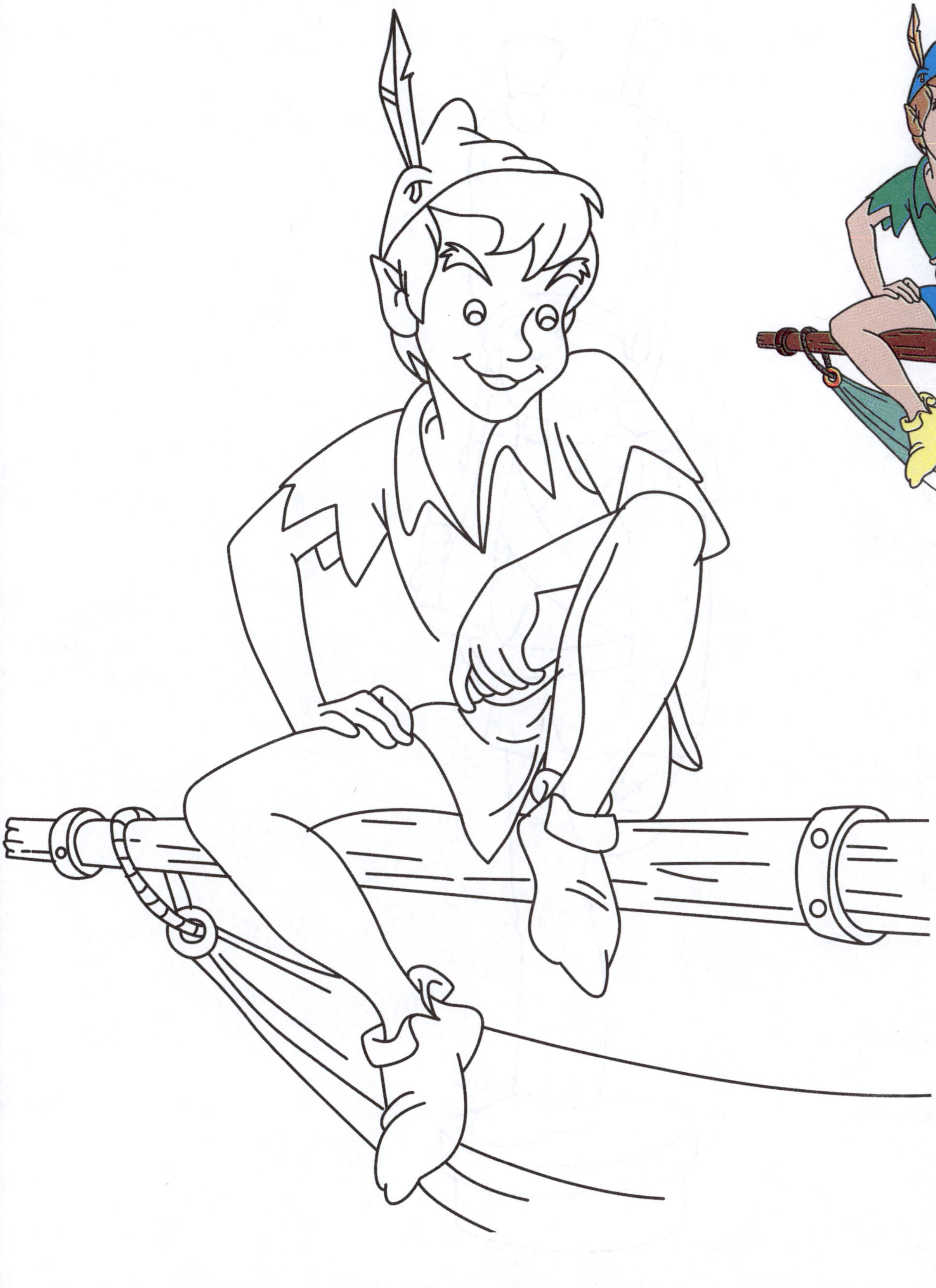

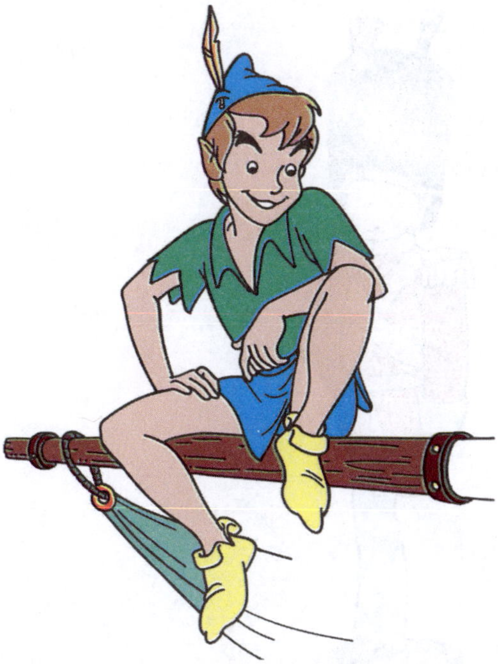

peter pan

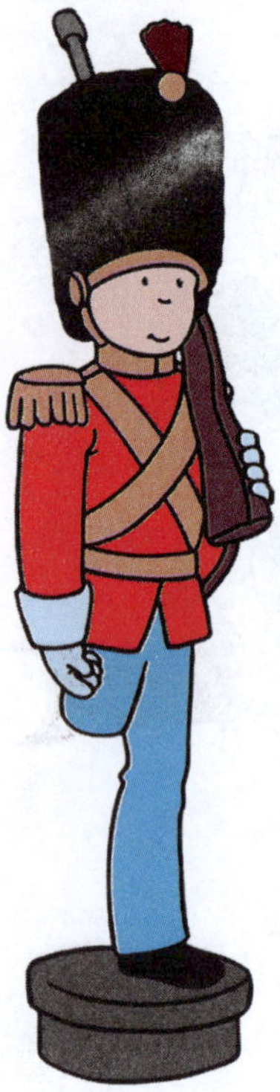

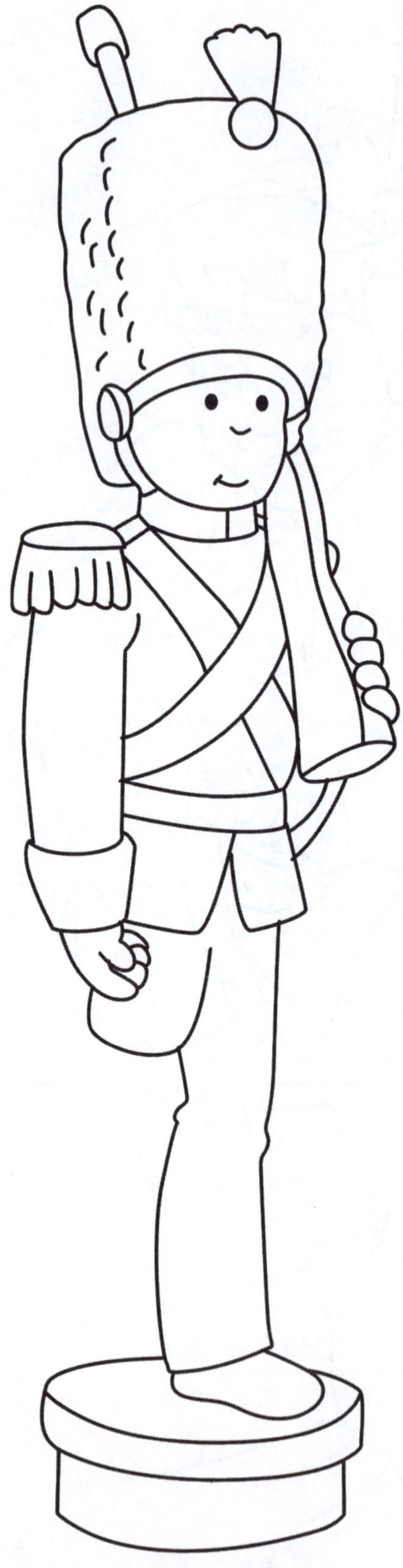

tin soldier

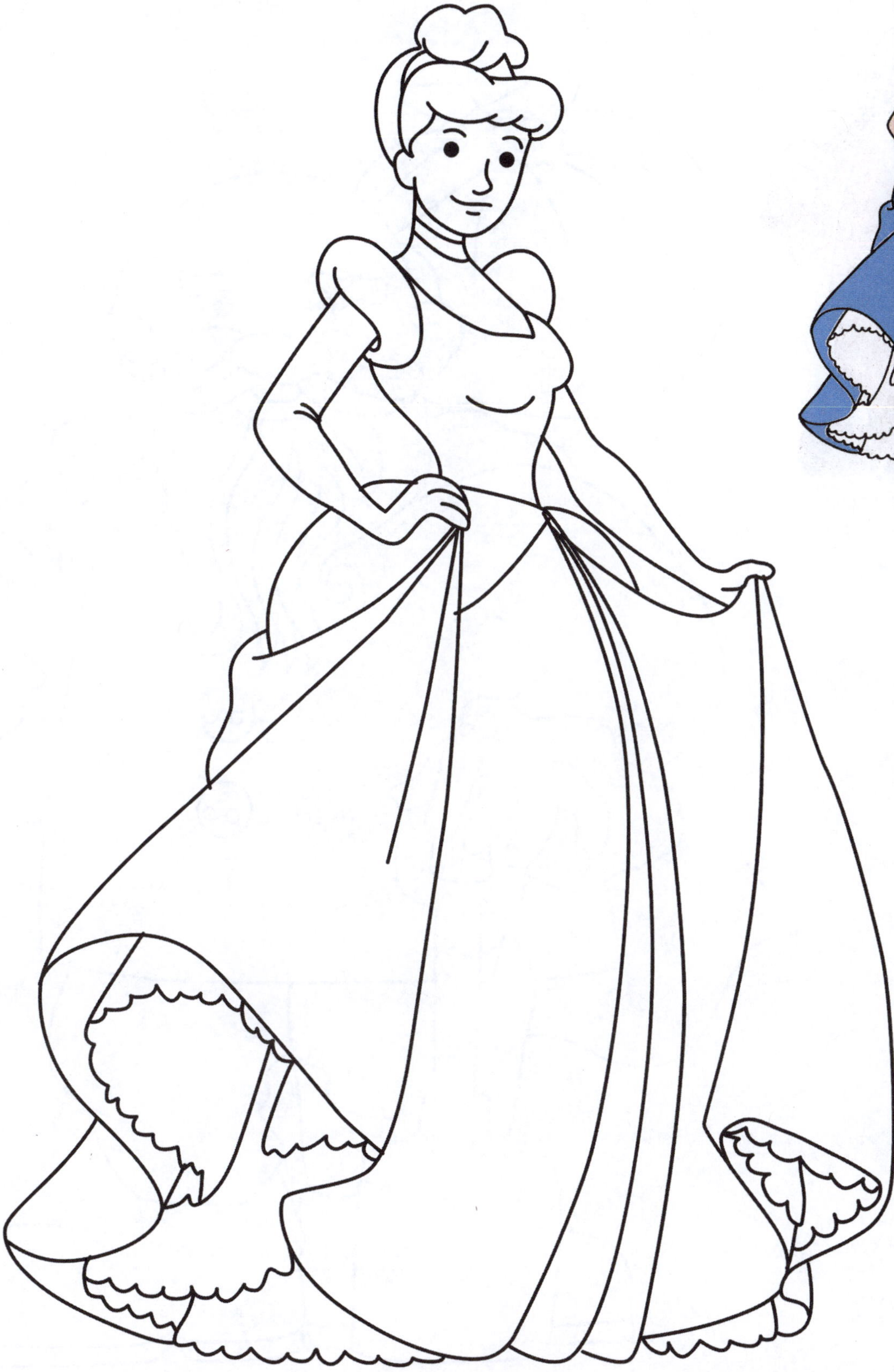

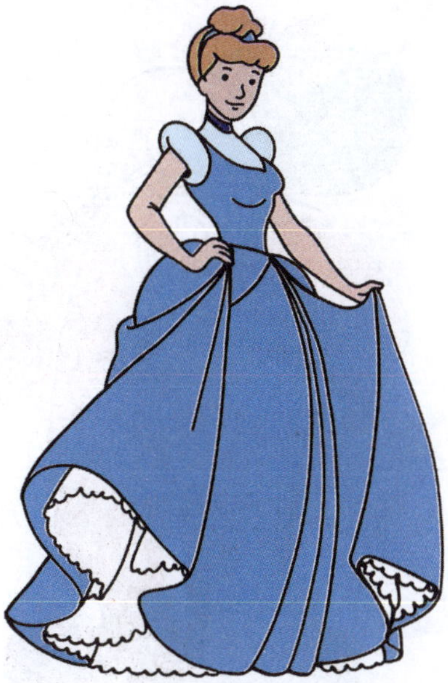

cinderella

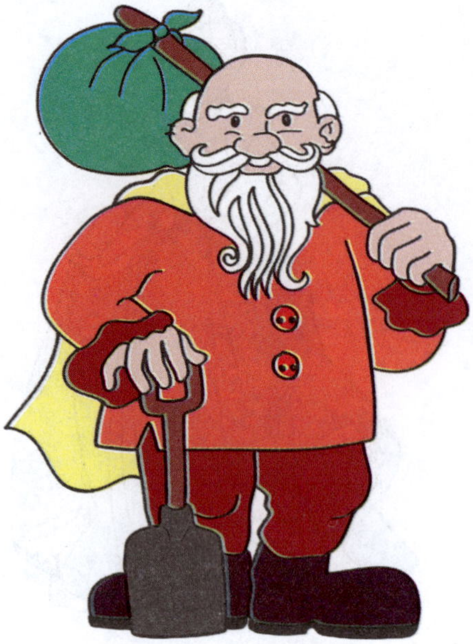

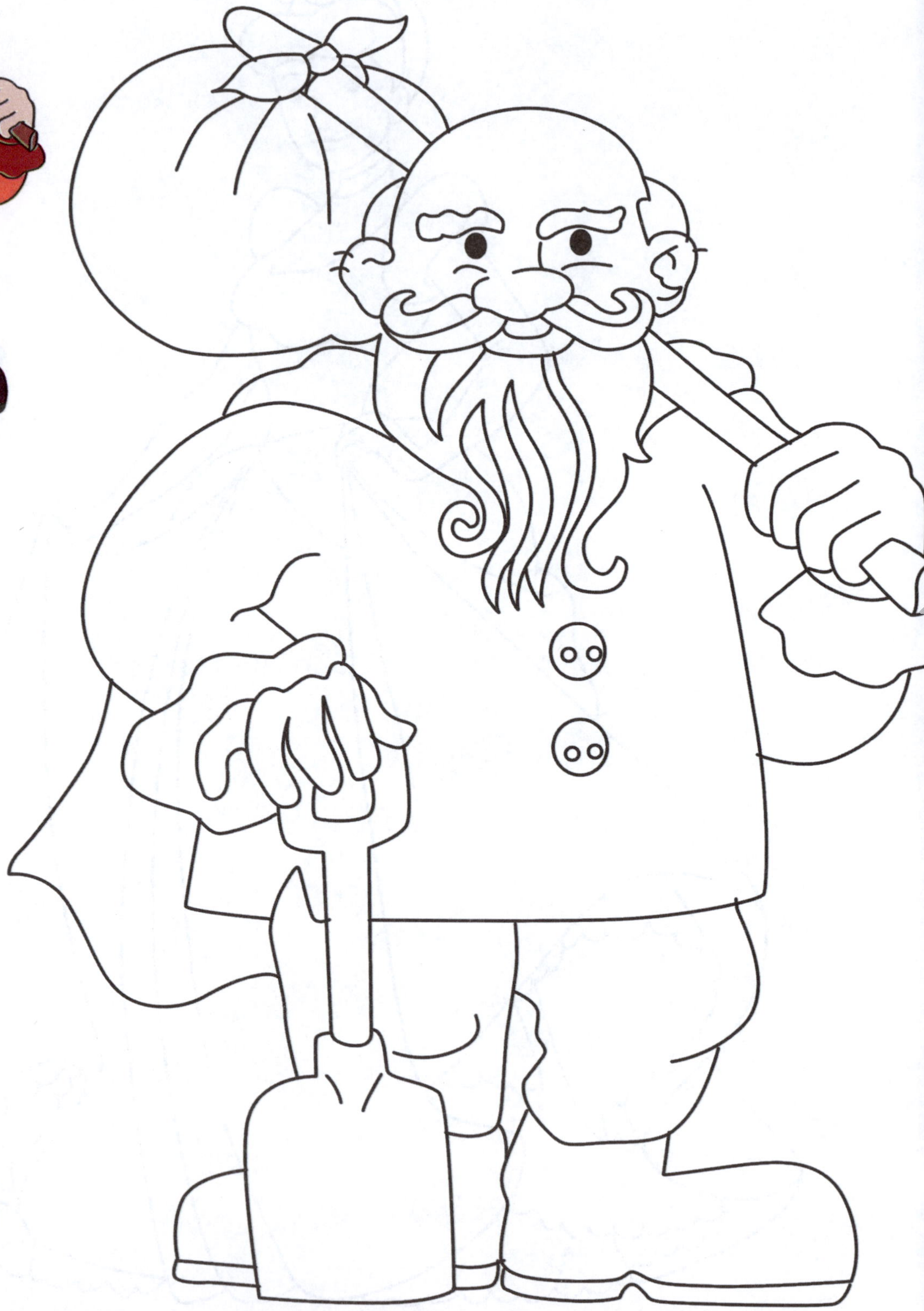

dwarf

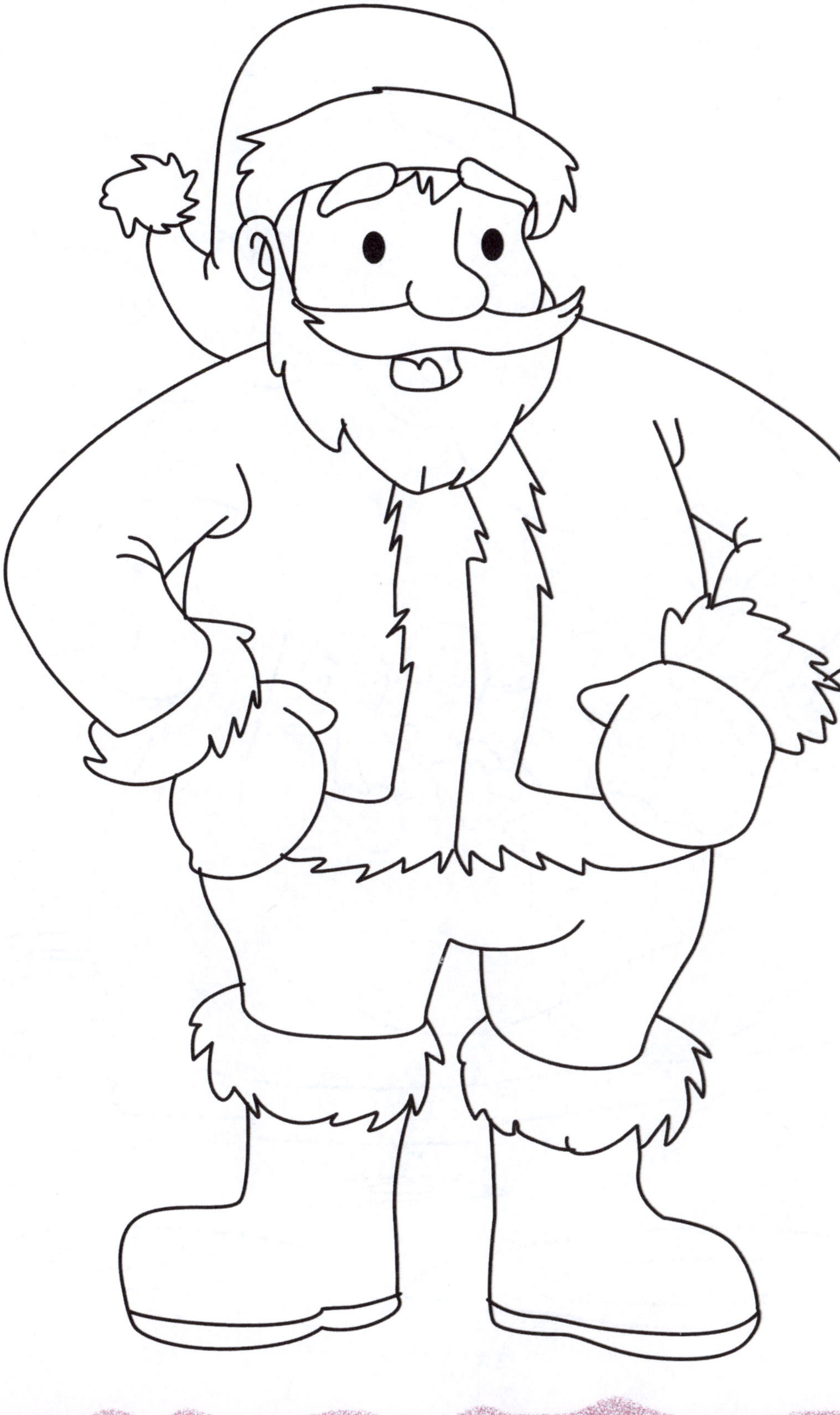

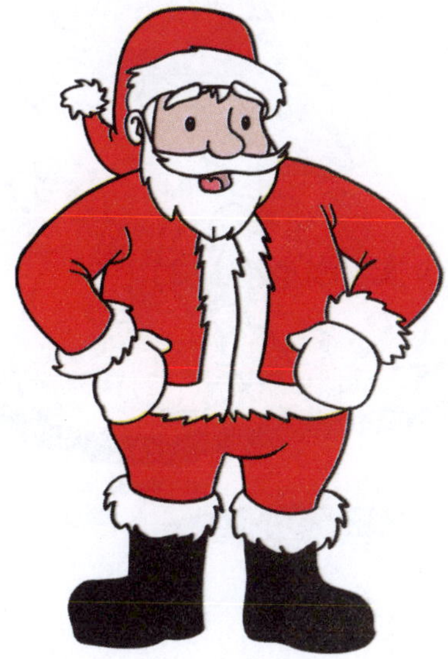

santa claus

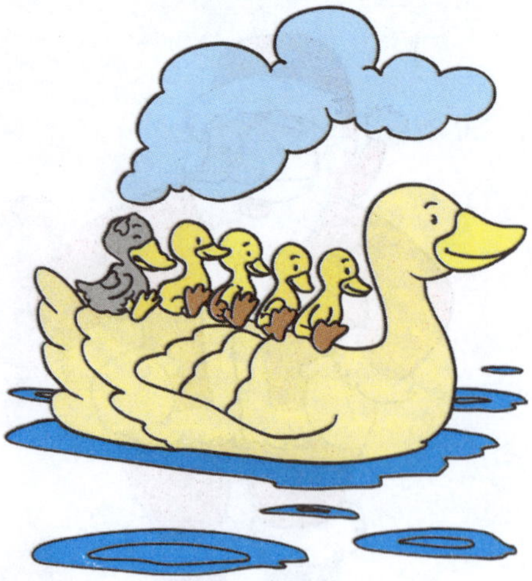

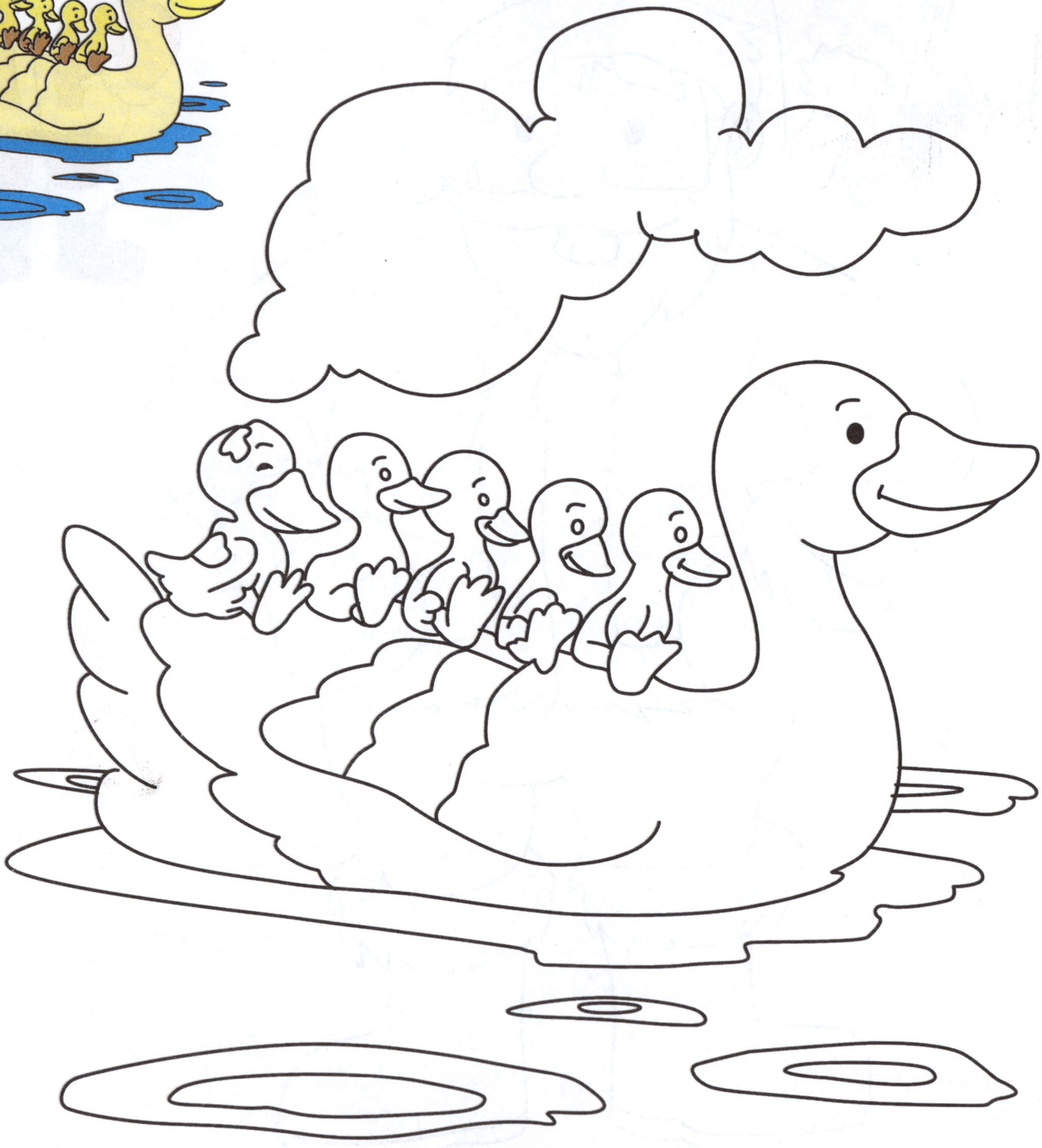

ugly duckling

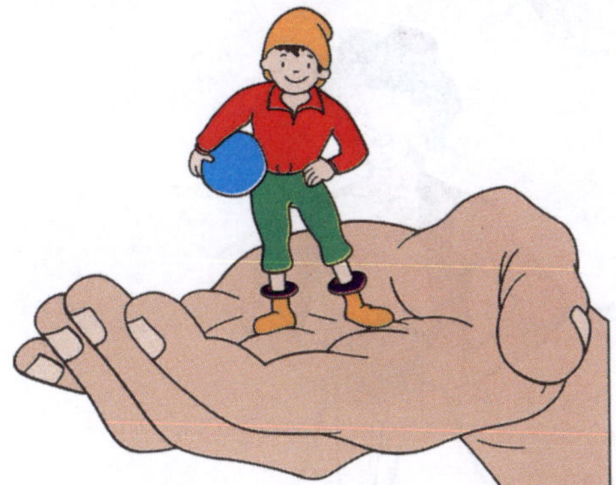

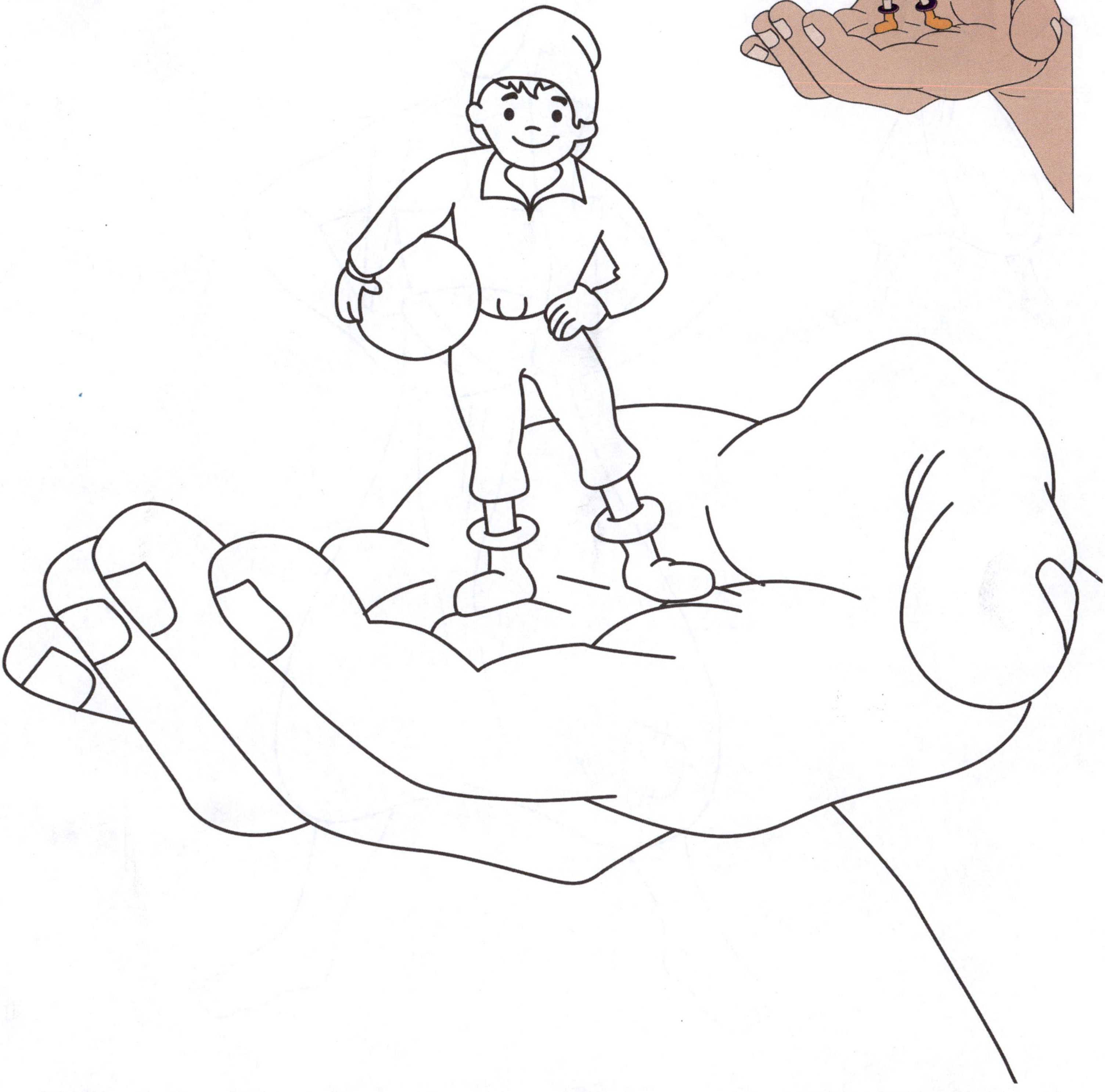

little tom thumb

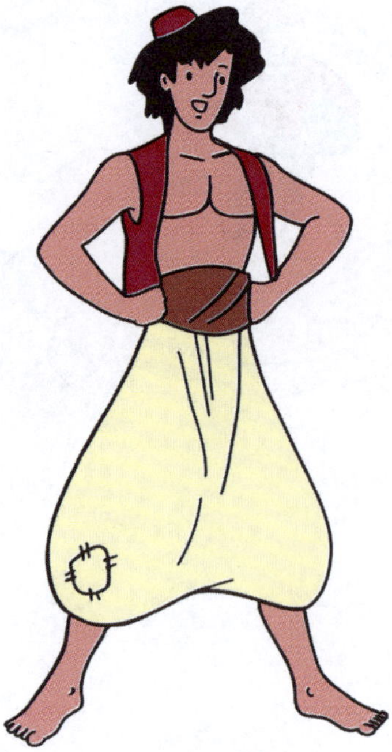

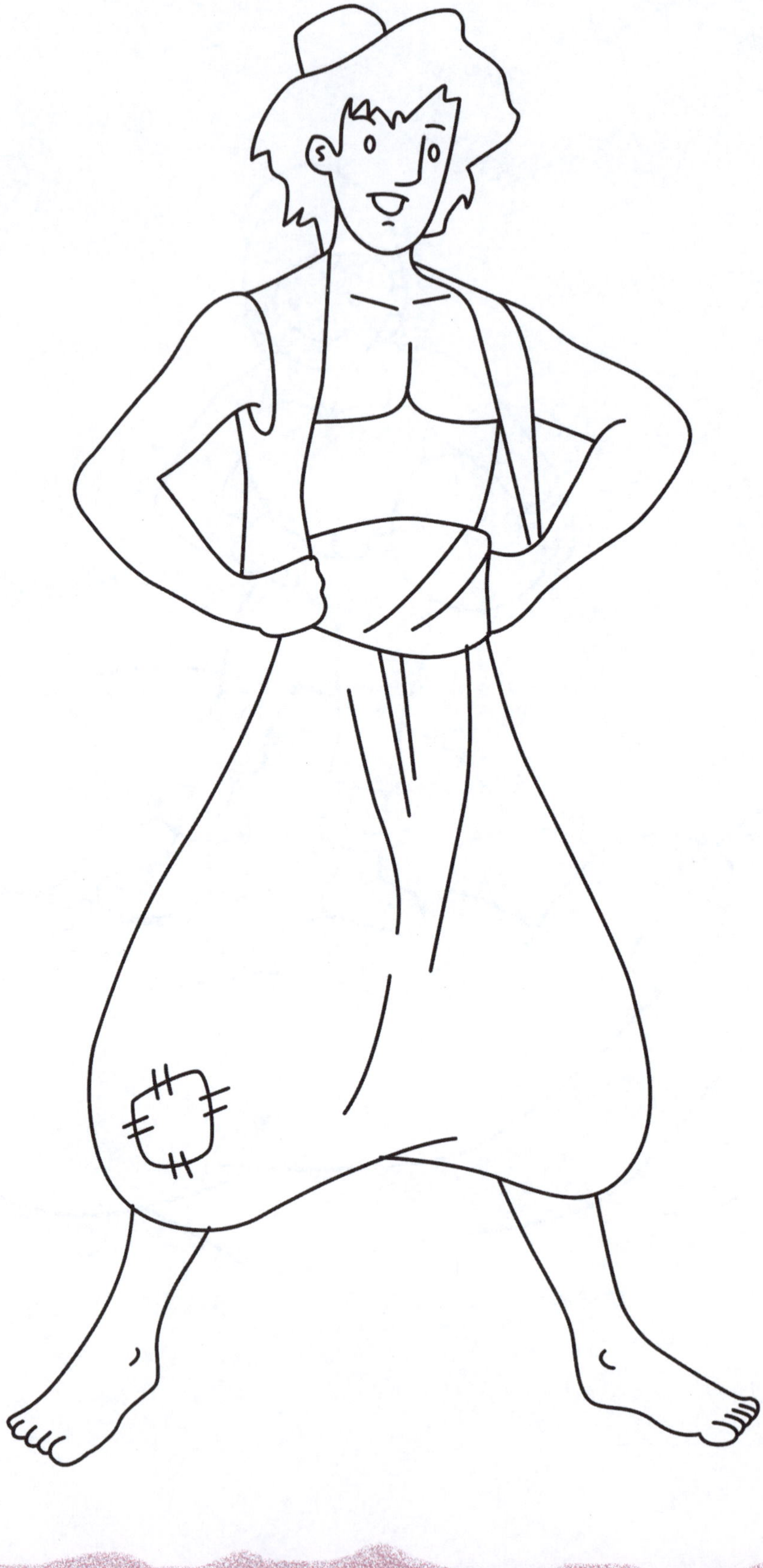

aladdin

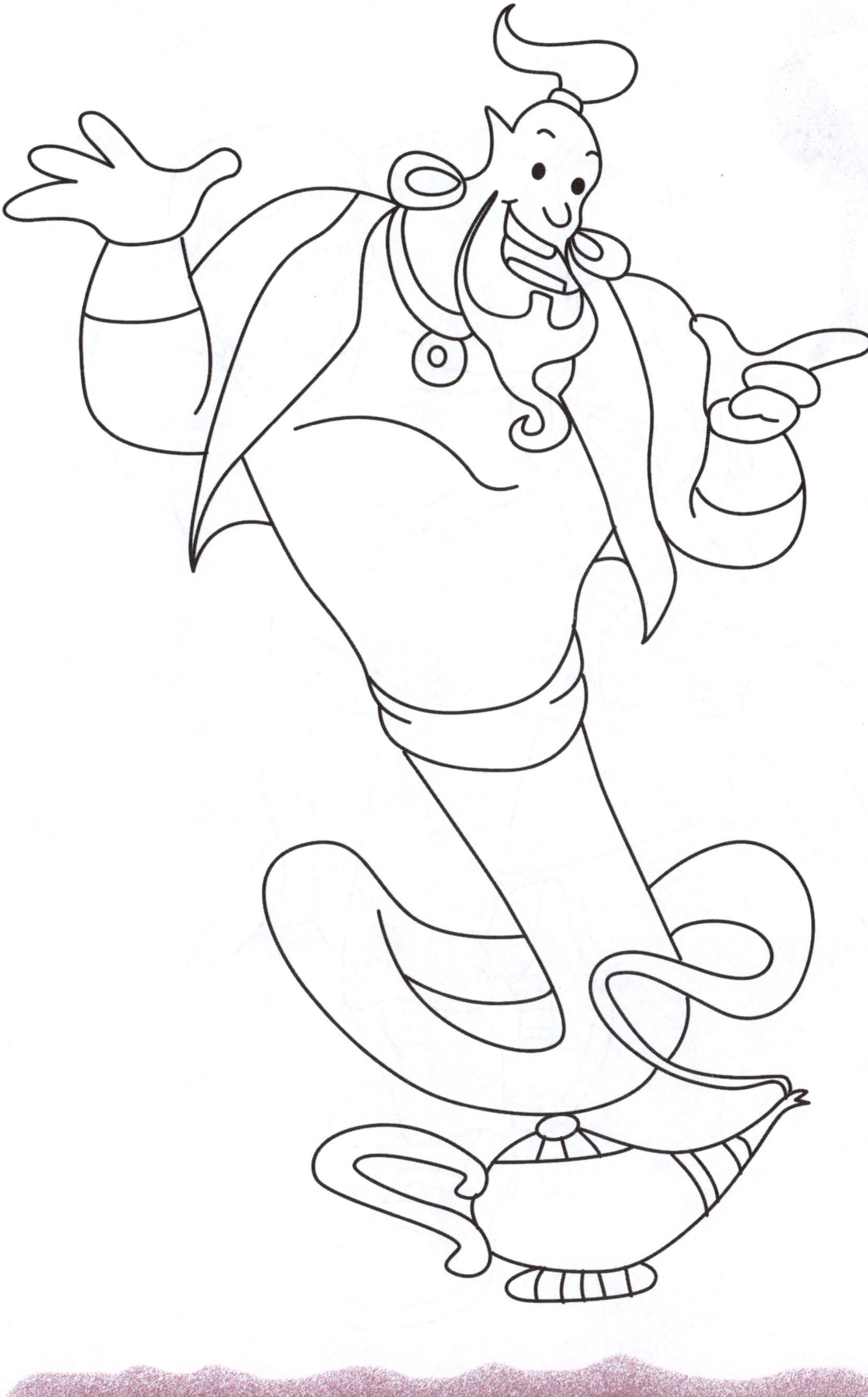

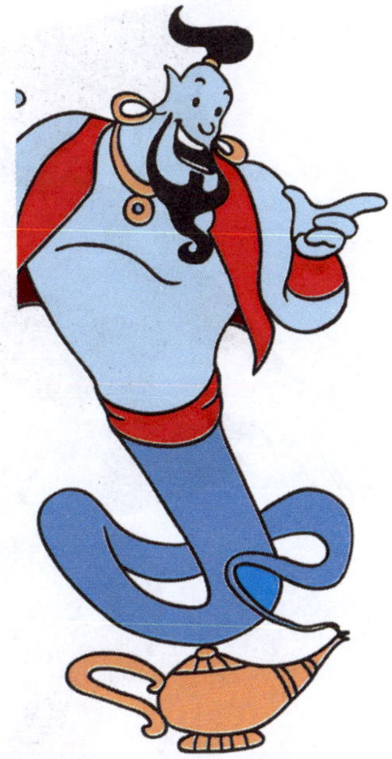

genie

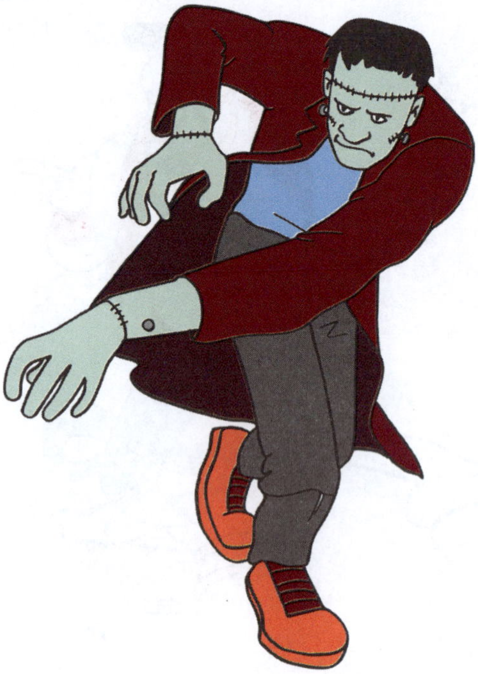

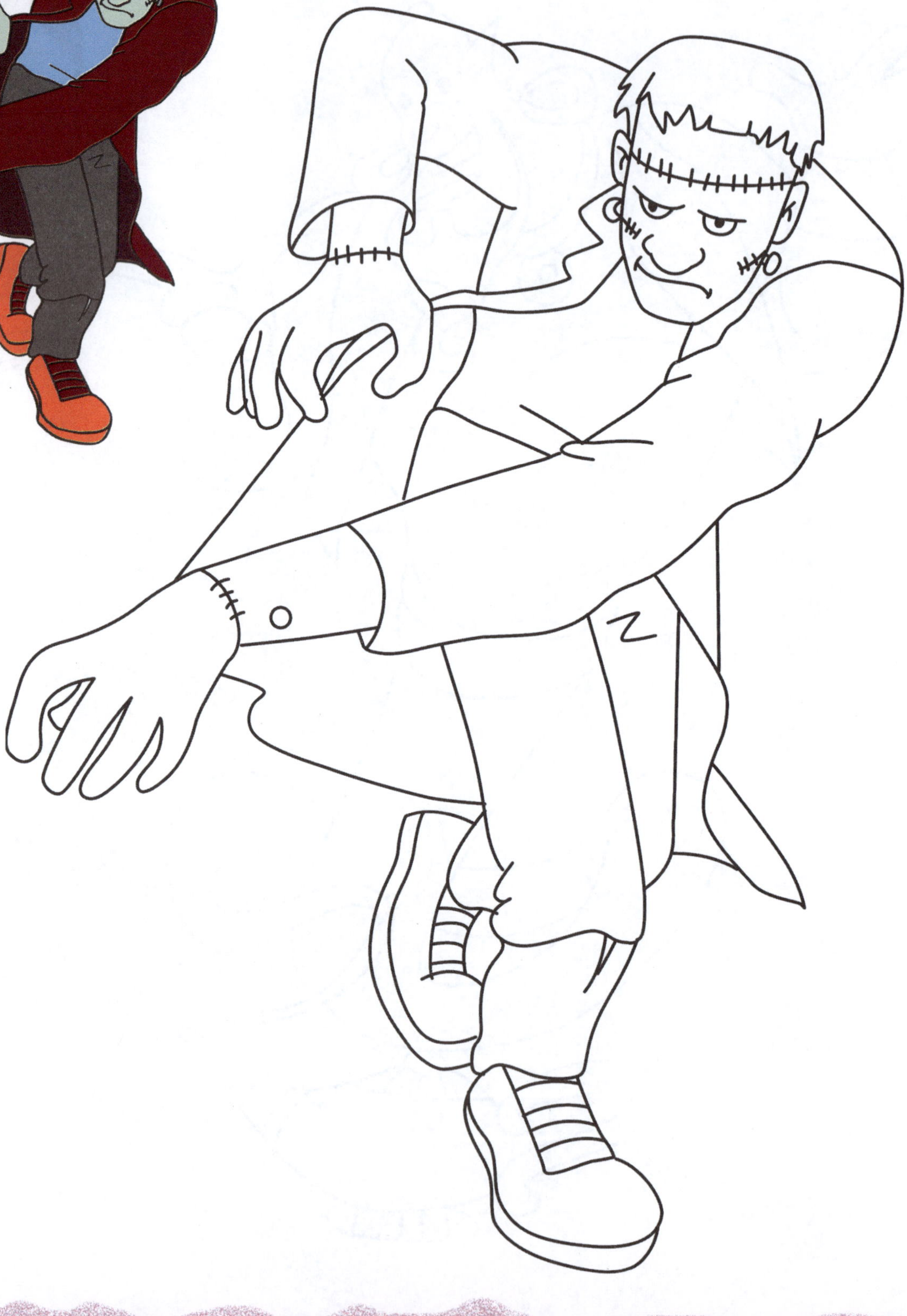

frankenstein

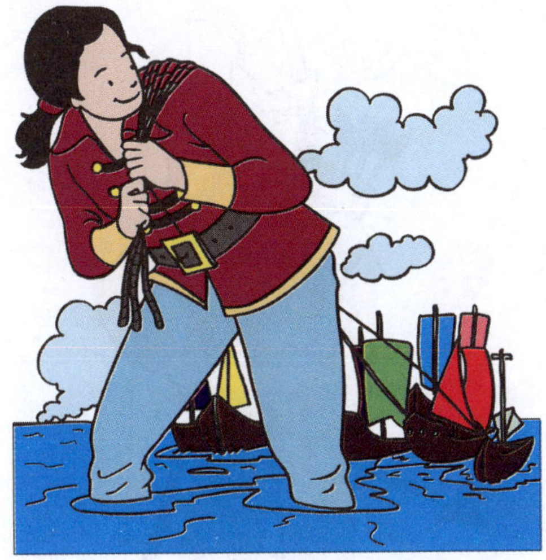

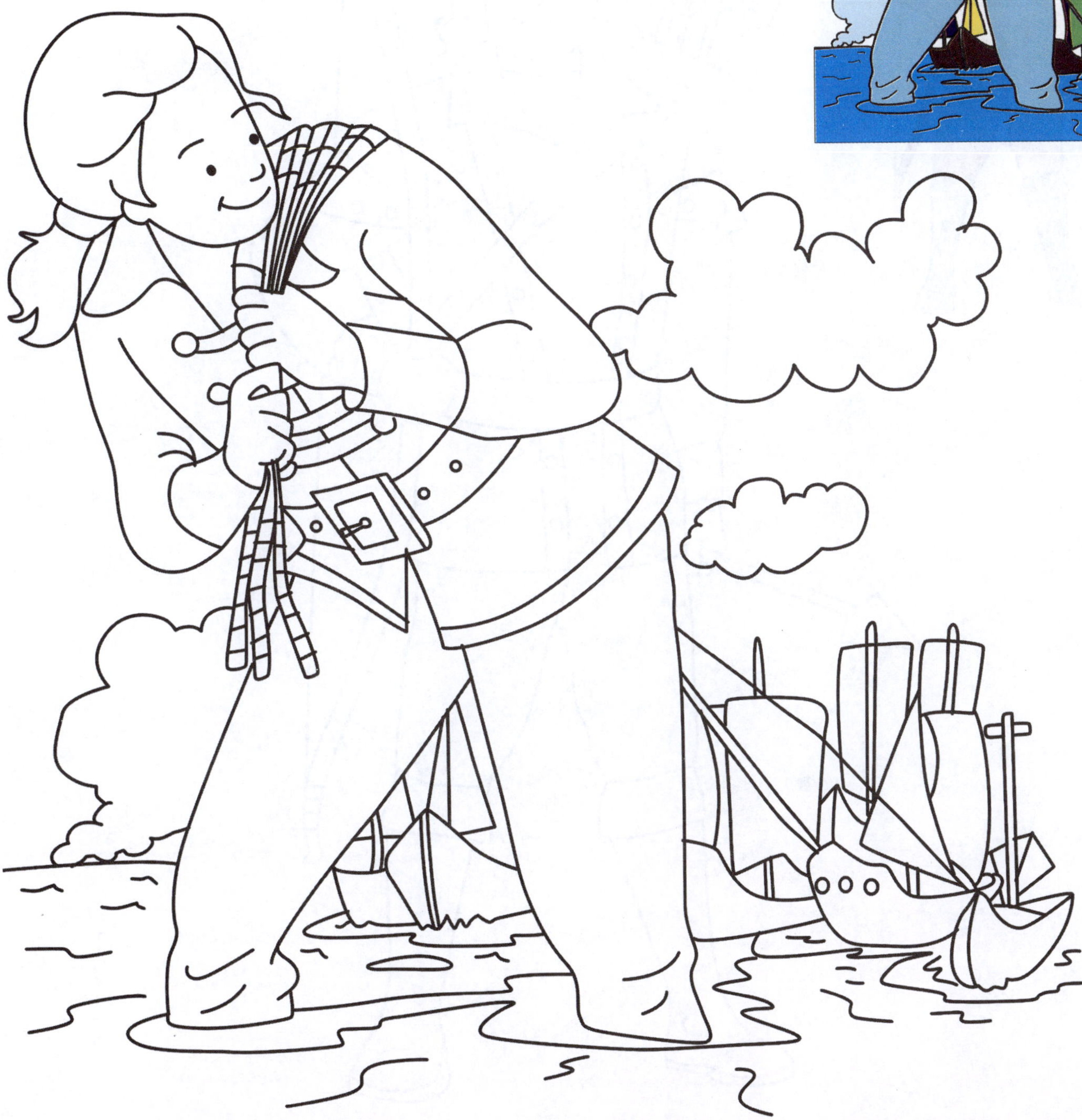

gulliver

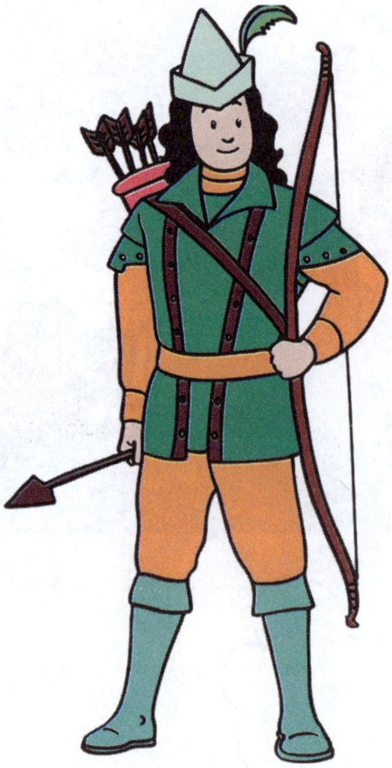

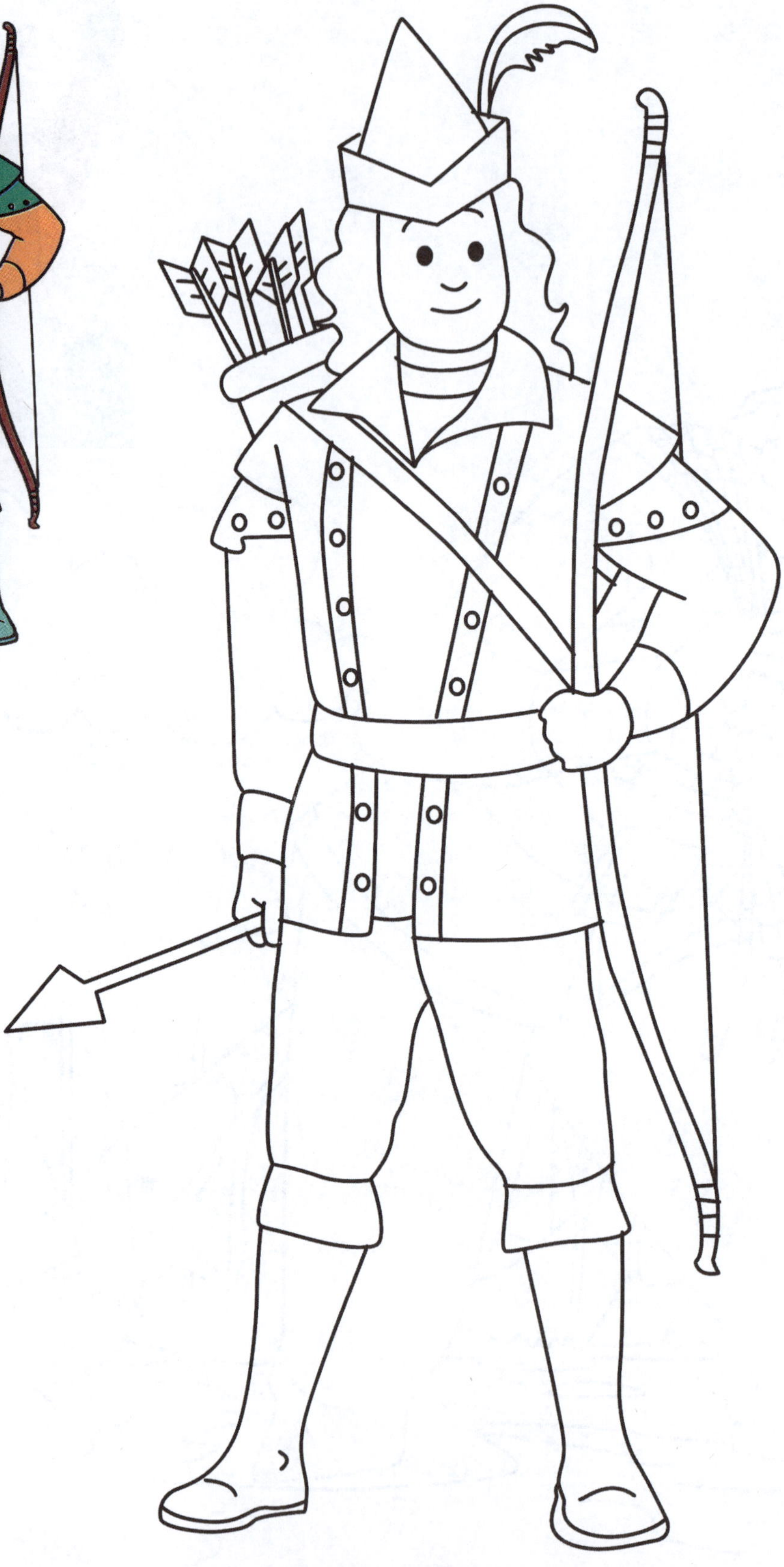

robin hood

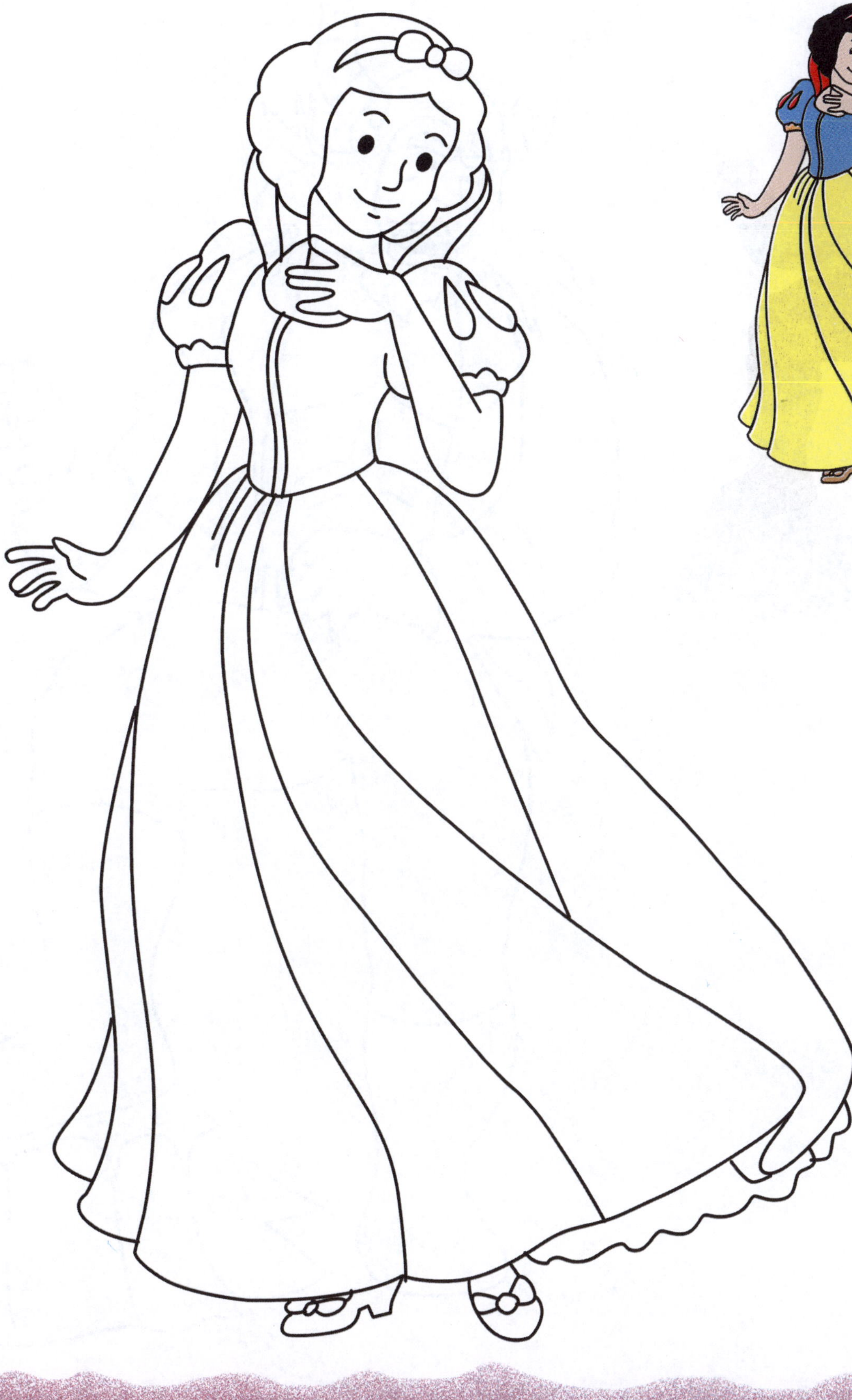

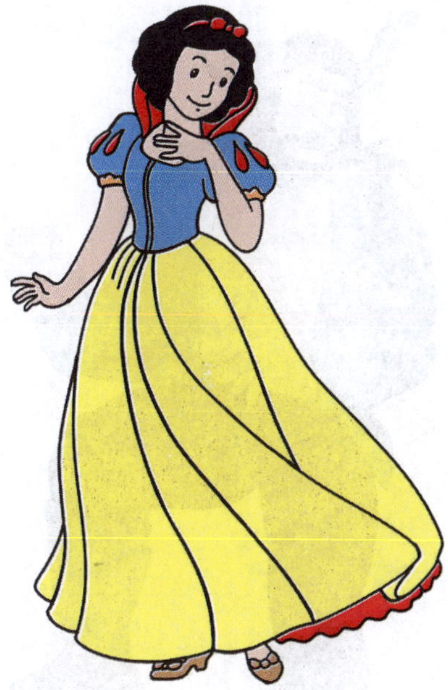

snow white

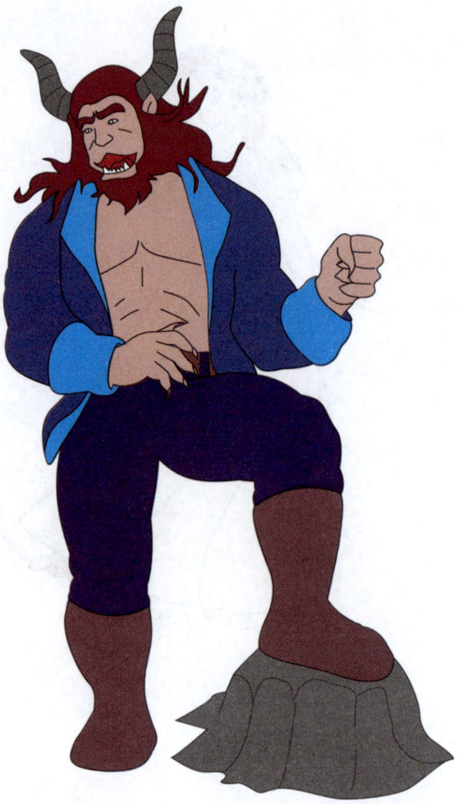

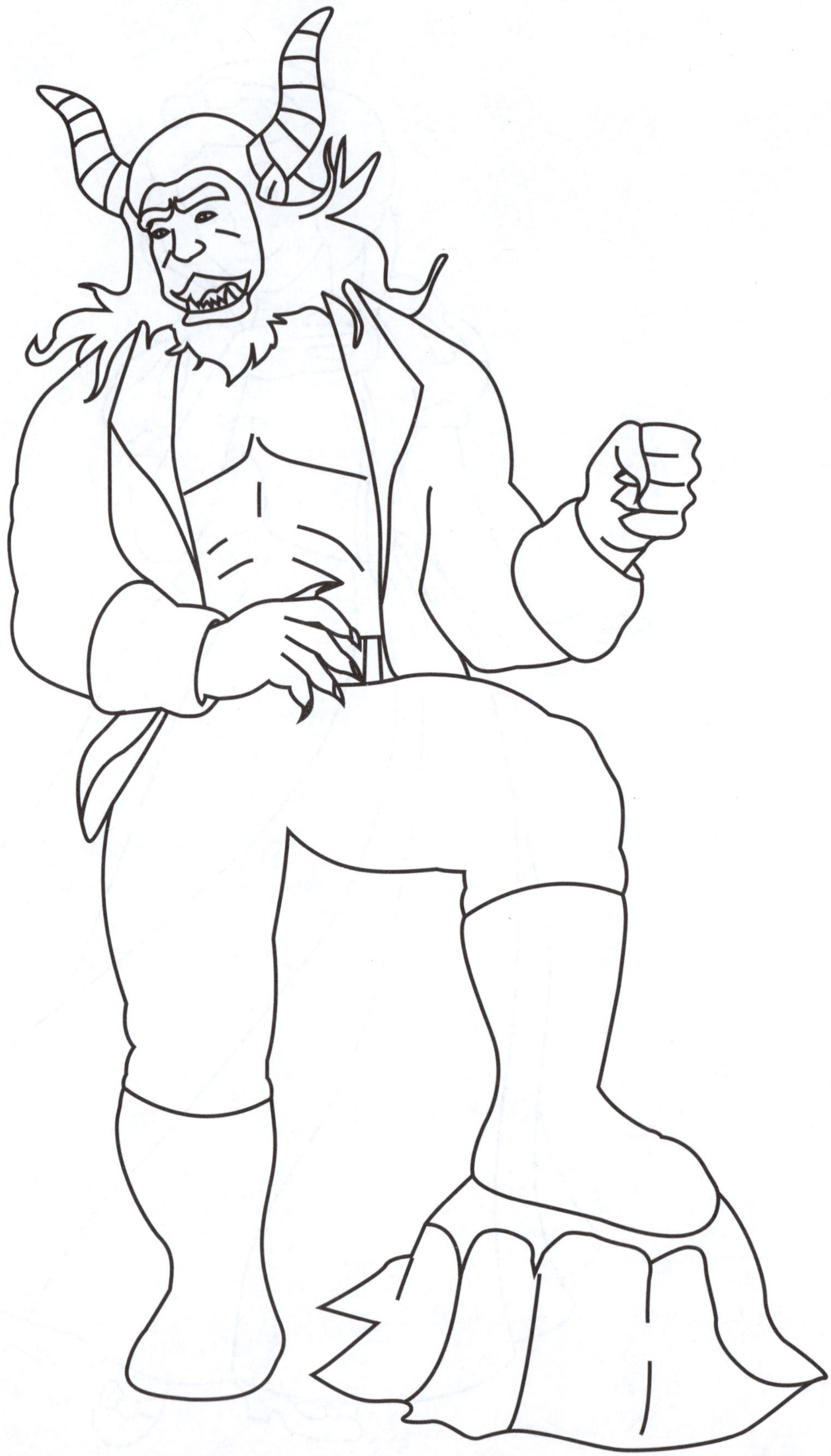

beast